Mom's Bed

Mom's Bed
Story by Elizabeth Busel
Illustrations by Katie Rissolo

Published by Hobo Jungle Press
Sharon, Connecticut, USA
St. Vincent & the Grenadines, W.I.

©2021 Elizabeth Busel/Katie Rissolo
First edition
Printed in the United States of America

ISBN 978-1-7331321-5-2

Library of Congress Control Number: 2021950848

Mom's Bed

by Elizabeth Busel

Illustrations by Katie Rissolo

This is Mom's bed.

It is good for lots of things.

We are fish and it is our pond.

We are wild animals hiding in a deep, dark cave.

We are circus performers and it is our trampoline.

We go camping and it is our tent.

We are Arctic explorers and it is our igloo.

We play hide and seek.

No one can ever find us.

We are the hosts of a grand tea party.

We are pirates searching for a buried treasure.

We are submarine commanders

moving slowly along the ocean floor.

We are famous rock stars and it is our stage.

We are the wrestling champions of the world.

We are cliff divers.

We are very tired!

This is Mom's bed.

It is good for lots of things.

But it is best with Mom in it.

CPSIA information can be obtained
at www.ICGtesting.com
Printed in the USA
LVHW070011260122
709433LV00002B/50